HOW TO
CHOOSE GOOD BOOKS
FOR KIDS

How to Choose
Good Books
for Kids

Kate Hall McMullan

Addison-Wesley Publishing Company
Reading, Massachusetts • Menlo Park, California
London • Amsterdam • Don Mills, Ontario • Sydney

In memory of my mother, who read me good books; and for my father, who read me the funnies.

Many thanks to the following people who helped me prepare this book: Paula Quint and Christine Stawicki of the Children's Book Council; Miriam Bernabei, Children's Librarian, Kips Bay, New York Public Library; Angeline Moscatt, Head Librarian, Donnell Central Children's Room, New York Public Library; Mrs. Jane Reutershan, Children's Librarian, East Hampton Library, Long Island, New York; Pam Hastings of The Corner Book Store; Holly Rivlin of Eeyore's Books for Children; Manny Rios and Ellen Marin of Barnes & Noble Bookstores; Emily Chewning, Linda Sunshine, Bina and Sarah Bernard; Jean, Danny, and David Marzollo; Vicky and Justin Stein; Susan and Jackson Whelen; Darleen, Leslie, and Jesse Lien; Tom Brokish; Cathee and Bruce Zebelle; Jane Levin; and, most of all, my resident reviewers, Jim and Leigh McMullan.

Library of Congress Cataloging in Publication Data

McMullan, Kate.
  How to choose good books for kids.

  Includes index.
  1. Children—Books and reading. 2. Libraries, Children's—Book selection. 3. School libraries—Book selection. 4. Bibliography—Best books—Children's stories. 5. Children's stories—Bibliography. I. Title.

Z1037.A1M385 1984   028.5′5   83-25840
ISBN 0-201-10809-7

Designed by Larry Kazal K.C. Witherell, New York
Set in 10 point Times Roman by Wendy B. Wolf

ABCDEFGHIJ-AL-87654
First printing, February 1984

CONTENTS

Note: In order to avoid the unwieldy "him or her" when referring to a child, I have chosen to give each sex a fair share of the language by using "him" and "her" in alternating chapters.

PREFACE

MOST OF THE TIPS given in the chapters that follow are for choosing good storybooks for kids, yet the criteria can easily apply to selecting good books for nonfiction, poetry, history, biography, even jokes and riddles – all types of books that combine to provide a balance of reading material. I have concentrated on works of fiction because it is stories that have the greatest possibility of reaching our emotions, of touching us, of enriching us with vivid, if vicarious, experiences in seeing life from different perspectives.

As I searched for good books to include in the annotated lists that appear at the end of each chapter, I spoke with teachers, librarians, booksellers, parents, and, most importantly, kids. I have tried to include as many books as possible that came to my attention directly from kids – kids who were really excited about them and wanted to share the good news. The other qualification for a book to be considered a "good book" was that it did what it set out to do well, with distinctive, individual style.

Because of the length of this book, I've had to leave off many wonderful books – there just wasn't space enough to include them all. So rather than being inclusive, this book should be considered a portable "starter set" in your search for good books for your kids.

PICKING OUT GOOD BOOKS for kids is important. With noted child development researchers such as Benjamin Bloom now concluding that children gain 50 percent of their intelligence by age four, and another 30 percent by age eight, it is our job as adults — parents, teachers, friends, uncles, aunts, librarians, writers, and editors — to give them something worthy to develop on, to grow on. And good books have it: strong characters to identify with; flowing, memorable language to absorb; vivid images to look at; exciting stories to ponder. It is, after all, the purpose of literature to develop and enrich the individual. This process can begin with the first good book you share with your child. Choosing good books for our children is a very special gift we can give them.

But it isn't an easy job, picking out good books — just the right books — for kids. A staggering number of new children's books roll off the printing presses each year — some 2,500 — and there are over 40,000 children's books already in print. Add to this total the thousands of out-of-print books that remain in library collections. Not even the most well-meaning parent or godparent can hope to sift through this quantity of books to find the ones of quality. It's no wonder that bookstores sell so many of the same old tried-and-true favorites by the same few authors, some of which were published thirty or forty years ago. At least they look familiar, and often reassuring, to present-day, book-buying adults. But, while many of the good old books are ones that shouldn't be missed, others have become dated. And, although the majority of books brought out each year are merely so-so or downright awful, some are treasures, well worth searching for.

INTRODUCTION

Sound too difficult? Take heart. There are some guidelines that can make picking out good children's books, both old and new, a less confusing ordeal and, quite possibly, a very satisfying endeavor.

1. *Consider the child for whom you are choosing the book.*
A child's age is a key. Sometimes the flap of a book jacket (or the back cover of a paperback) will give an indication of the age range the publisher feels the book is for. This can be helpful, but don't feel restricted by it. Beware of picking out a book that looks too babyish for a child, but don't worry about picking one intended for a slightly older child, particularly in the case of a gift book. This way, a child can "grow into" the book, and it can have a long span of appreciation. Browse with your child in bookstores and libraries to get a sense of his tastes. His interests, fears, and passions can all guide you.

2. *Pick books that you like.*
After all, until your child is well into elementary school and perhaps for years after that, it is you who will read the books to him over and over again. If you are bored by a book that you are reading to your child, you will pass that message on to him, and he may decide that reading is a bore. If, on the other hand, you are really tickled or touched by a passage in a book, you will pass on your honest enjoyment to your child, coupling the pleasure of a good story with the pleasure of sharing it.

3. *Take a good, hard look at a book you are considering.*
Read some of the text. Does the language have a pleasing rhythm and flow? Have the words been chosen with care? Is it something that you would enjoy reading aloud? Flip through the book to get a sense of the characters, story, and theme. Is there enough "food for thought" so that the book will satisfy throughout many readings and last a long time? If it is a picture book, be aware of your reactions to the illustrations. Are they rich and vigorous? Full of special detail? Do they have images and colors that you would like your child to look at again and again? If the answer to any of these questions is a firm *no*, then you probably shouldn't buy this book.

4. *Patronize a bookstore that takes children's books seriously.*
A good children's book section has books arranged in a logical way so that you can easily find the kind of book you are looking for. It should also have

a salesperson handy who really knows children's books and can make some good recommendations. Often, bookstores have special programs for kids, with a storyteller, puppet show, or author's visit. Ask for information about these. If the bookstore nearest you doesn't come up to standard, perhaps your interest as a potential book buyer can make a difference.

5. *Visit the library often.*
As soon as a child can print his own name, he can get a library card of his own. This is terrific incentive for reading. Since many research studies have shown that parents who like to read have children who are good readers, trips to the library, where both parent and child come home with some good books, reinforce the value of reading to a child. At the library, you can practice picking out good children's books without feeling pressure to buy. And if your child insists that a particular book is a must but you're not so sure, checking it out of the library can give it a two-week trial run. Libraries often display new books and publish their own lists and reviews of books that are worth considering, and many children's librarians are quite skilled at matching the right book to the right child.

6. *Get to know some reference books to help you find books by subject.*
If your five-year-old, for example, has devoured all the books in your library and local bookstore on dinosaurs, and he's ready for more, ask the bookseller to direct you to *A Subject Guide to Children's Books in Print*, which lists children's books by topic. A bookseller can take an order for a book you find in the *Subject Guide* and get it directly from the publisher. (The books sometimes take a few weeks to come in, so don't wait until the day before a birthday to place an order.) Another excellent guide is *A to Zoo: Subject Access to Children's Picture Books* by Carolyn Lima (Bowker, 1982). These references can also be helpful to parents looking for books dealing with problem situations, such as the first day of school or the death of a pet. Often booksellers and librarians will have their own lists of "bibliotherapy" books to recommend.

7. *Get to know the names of some authors of books that your child likes.*
Chances are pretty good that if your child is enthusiastic about one book by a particular author, he'll enjoy another. Many authors write series of books, using the same cast of characters from book to book, which are very popu-

lar with middle graders, or write books within a particular genre, such as mystery or science fiction.

8. *Check book club offerings carefully.*

Many seductive ads get the attention of parents with young children by using words like *learning* and *reading* in their headlines. But read the small print, too. A good book club for children, like the reputable clubs for adults, gives you a choice of books to order each month. Be aware of just what you will need to do to cancel a home subscription. Some companies make it purposely difficult to return books, hoping that parents will find it easier simply to keep the books coming. This is one way for your child to accumulate a big library, but it might be full of books he never cares about reading. When you make the extra effort to pick out good books for your kids, you're also doing yourself a favor: you can appreciate a well-written story and handsome illustrations while simultaneously enjoying your children's involvement in the book. Even books for very young children can provide this dual pleasure. From the age of seventeen months until she was about two years old, my daughter Leigh asked to hear Margaret Wise Brown's *The Little Fur Family* nearly every night before bed. I never grew tired of reading it to her because the language is fresh and original, the stuff of poetry:

> *There was a little fur family*
> *warm as toast*
> *smaller than most*
> *in little fur coats*
> *and they lived in a warm wooden tree.*

Garth Williams's illustrations show, in soft colors and touching detail, the daily lives of the little fur creatures, and the story is about as warm and full of love and security as a story can be. When my daughter and I read this story, we were sharing in all that warmth and love. And we share it still, even though we read the book only occasionally now, a year later. Leigh sometimes asks for the lullaby that closes the book for her goodnight song. When she sneezes, I often find myself quoting the old fur grandpa, saying, "Bless you, my little fur child. Every time you sneeze." This story has become a part of us, has enriched our lives and our relationship. And it is this resonance — the ability of a story to continue to reverberate within us long after the reading experience is over — that reading good books is all about.

1
First Books
Birth through 2 years

SOME PEOPLE BELIEVE that it's never too early to introduce good books to children. A friend of mine went so far as to read only classic Russian novels during her pregnancy in the hopes that a love of fine literature would be instilled in her baby-to-be. She gave birth to a healthy baby girl who, at an early age, showed great affection for books and reading time. I'm not saying there's a cause-and-effect relationship here, but I'm not scoffing, either.

Most people are content to wait until some time after the births of their babies to begin reading to them, yet many begin reading aloud right away. If you think about it from an infant's point of view, it makes sense to do this. During her first year of life, a baby's biggest job is to begin decoding our spoken language and to begin speaking it herself to make her needs known. A baby can learn language only from listening. When you read or sing to a baby, the language that she hears becomes a part of the material that she has to work with.

An excellent source of vigorous language for baby to grown on is Mother Goose rhymes. These rhymes have stood the test of time and have a rich vocabulary and lilting rhythms that please a baby. Mother Goose rhymes repeat a line over and over, which helps a baby learn to anticipate the line and then to remember it. Also, the rhymes seem to cover every event in a baby's life, from waking up to going to sleep. It's hard to imagine anything more perfectly designed for a baby's first two years than the rhymes of Mother Goose.

A good collection of Mother Goose is an excellent way to begin baby's library. (And it can serve as a reference for parents who get stuck on a rhyme

FIRST BOOKS

they thought they knew!) A Mother Goose anthology can have a long life if it is selected with care.

- It should be comprehensive enough to contain some very simple rhymes for baby, and some more complex rhymes to grow on. The traditional rhymes should be there and so much the better if it has a few good rhymes that are less well known.
- The large-format editions with one rhyme per page, illustrated with one big, bright, clear picture are appreciated by babies just old enough to sit in a lap and look and listen at the same time. As the rhymes and pictures become old friends, two- and three-year-olds who have memorized them take great pleasure in showing that they can "read" all the words on the page of a great big book.
- A sturdily constructed book can survive to be read by child after child for years.
- Some parents like to have a large anthology for the home and a smaller, portable Mother Goose that can travel in a stroller bag on errands or to the doctor's office.

Another good first book for a baby is a songbook. Like a Mother Goose collection, a songbook can have many years of steady use.

- Select a songbook that has nursery favorites plus songs for the older child.
- Pictures in a songbook for a young child should not be simply decorations, but should offer images that provide a visual counterpoint to the songs.

At about six months of age, many babies can sit up alone. This leaves their hands free for holding and examining things, and some parents have found that this is a good time to give the baby her first small book. Cloth books, popular a generation ago with the diaper set, are apt to frustrate a young child because they droop and are difficult to hold in true book-fashion. The best bet for a first book is a small "board book" of eight or ten pages, printed on sturdy cardboard and laminated with a clear, nontoxic, wipe-clean surface. But, because many a baby will still judge a book by its cover — and how well it serves as a teething tool — it is important to give your baby safe books as well as good books. Some things to check for are:

- solid construction that will stand up to hard use
- rounded corners, not sharp ones

FIRST BOOKS

- no parts that could easily be pulled off and swallowed
- if spiral-bound, books should not have exposed metal or plastic points that could scratch.

With infants, the sound of the words is the key element to the enjoyment of a book, but as a baby grows old enough to focus her attention on pictures, illustrations become equally important. During the first two years of a baby's life, her visual perception is just developing. It takes her a while to make sense of the real objects she sees in her world, and being able to look at a two-dimensional representation of those objects on a page of a book is a big step forward in perception. When you are selecting a baby's first picture books, look for the following:

- pictures that stand out clearly from an uncluttered background
- simple pictures without too much going on in them
- pictures of whole objects (Babies can be confused by seeing just a part of an object and disturbed by seeing something with a part missing.)
- realistic art or clear photographs rather than abstract or very stylized pictures
- a thoughtfully designed book
- interesting pictures that *you* like looking at

First little books are probably wise to purchase rather than check out of a library. This way, your librarian won't be upset when you return books with gnawed corners, and your baby won't be exposed to any germy books. (There are those who claim that giving a baby a pacifier while she looks at a book will lessen the chances of the book entering her mouth, but this never worked for me.) Also, many children love their "old favorite" board books for years to come, so you'll want to have them around, even if, eventually, you have to keep their separate pages in a box!

But before too long, your baby will stop putting everything into her mouth and paper ripping will have lost its charm. Now you can sit down with her and read a book with thin paper pages. For this age, from about one year to two years, the key to success with books is participation.

- When a baby begins to imitate sounds she hears, she is likely to have fun with books that call for making the sounds of animals, cars, musical instruments, almost anything noisy.
- When a baby reaches out to touch things, she is ready for "feely"

books. These books ask babies to rub a stubby finger on a variety of different textures, while the text uses words to describe them.

- Another favorite way for a child to interact with a book is to "point and say." At this stage, a child is learning the names of all the things that surround her in the world, and books that expand on this desire to name are very popular with babies.

At around two years of age, children begin to use language to form mental images, to get what they want, and to test what happens when they say, "No!" Twos are on the move, trying to grab, sniff, taste, and seemingly destroy everything in their path. They want to know about everything and exhaust their parents with a constant stream of "Why? Why? Why?" Yet it is difficult to explain anything to a two-year-old because she is able to concentrate her fleeting attention on just one aspect of an object at a time, and her point of view is totally self-centered. It's no wonder that a parent's patient explanation often leads only to another puzzled, "Why?"

Books can be very helpful to a child in the throes of "terrible twoness." They can answer some of the *whys* and they can help her explore the world vicariously — without making a mess for once. Of course, two-year-olds need primary, hands-on experience in manipulating things in order to learn, and books are no substitute for it, but they can enhance firsthand experience. And books can be used in a way that can mean a great deal to a toddler: they can slow down the world and, for a moment, make it go at a comprehensible, two-year-old pace. Real life is hard to stop when a child has a question, and TV just keeps moving right along, but a two-year-old can easily stop someone who is reading her a book and ask questions about what she doesn't understand until she is satisfied. A book can be read at any speed.

Storybooks for two-year-olds may seem a bit dull to parents perusing them in a library or bookstore, but don't be put off. Test a few of the books recommended in this chapter with a child, and you'll begin to realize that to her, the mundane is terribly interesting. To paraphrase G. K. Chesterton, a child of seven is excited by being told that Tommy opened the door and saw a dragon, but a very young child is excited by being told that Tommy opened the door!

- Stories for twos need to be very straightforward, with one story line which moves right along to a warm, satisfying conclusion. Sad endings can be upsetting.

- Any attempts at humor must be geared to a two-year-old sense of what is funny. Books aimed primarily at the adult chuckle are out of place.
- The characters in stories, be they humans or humans in animal guise, need to behave in predictable ways.
- A warm central character for a child to identify with can make a book very special to a two-year-old.
- Familiar characters, such as the *Sesame Street* Muppets, are popular with kids.
- Like the rest of us, young children enjoy variety in their reading material: stories told in rhyme and those told in prose; realistic stories and stories that are make-believe.
  As you flip through books in a library or bookstore, ask yourself:
- Are the illustrations clear and easy to understand?
- Are there just a few words per page?
- Are there pictures on every spread of pages?
- Are there ways for my child to participate with this book? Can she make noises? Complete rhyming couplets? Act out the story? Find a hidden picture? At this age, the more senses a child can use to explore a story, the more meaning it will have.

Good First Books
Mother Goose

THE BABY'S LAP BOOK
collected and illustrated by Kay Chorao
Dutton, 1977
- Soft black-and-white illustrations on pages bordered in delicious pastel colors set off familiar and less familiar rhymes. A lovely gift book.

CHINESE MOTHER GOOSE RHYMES
edited by Robert Wyndham
illustrated by Edward Young
World, 1968; Philomel paperback
- Translations of traditional Chinese rhymes prove to be very much like our English versions. The book opens vertically and is illustrated with batik-like pictures, which will appeal to a child of two and up.

FIRST BOOKS

MOTHER GOOSE
illustrated by Tasha Tudor
McKay, 1944

■ Lovely drawings, one to a page, accompany 77 rhymes. This book is big enough for lap reading, but not too big to be held comfortably by a toddler. Also by Tudor for this age group: *Tasha Tudor's Five Senses*.

THE REAL MOTHER GOOSE
illustrated by Blanche Fisher Wright
Rand, 1916

■ Recently reissued, this book holds more than 400 verses, and the illustrations are brightly colored and easy to understand. A good choice for young children. (Selections from this big book are available in *The Real Mother Goose Husky Books*, Vols. One and Two, which are printed on sturdy cardboard for babies.)

THE TALL BOOK OF MOTHER GOOSE
illustrated by Feodor Rojankovsky
Harper, 1942

■ Favorite rhymes, one per page, are illustrated with bold, clear pictures, which alternate full-color and black-and-white. The long, skinny format of the book makes it unusual and easy for a toddler to manage.

Songbooks

THE GOLDEN SONG BOOK
edited by Katharine Tyler Wessells
illustrated by Kathy Allert
Western, 1981

■ Here are pleasant, clear pictures accompanying the traditional songs, along with music for piano and guitar. Suggestions for games and activities that go with many of the songs are given. A hands-on kids' book.

FIRST BOOKS

THE GREAT SONG BOOK
edited by Timothy John
illustrated by Tomi Ungerer
music edited by Peter Hankey
Doubleday, 1978

■　A large volume of over 60 songs from traditional sources is divided into sections such as Songs of Dance and Play and Evening Songs and Lullabies. Ungerer's spirited and lusty artwork adds a sophistication and humor to this book that will insure its popularity well past nursery days.

LULLABIES AND NIGHT SONGS
edited by William Engvack
illustrated by Maurice Sendak
music by Alec Wilder
Harper & Row, 1965

■　Songs to lull baby to sleep as well as songs to "end the day with a laugh" are richly, gorgeously illustrated in this big book, which includes traditional songs and some lovely poems set to music for the first time. You'll find William Blake's "Cradle Song," Robert Louis Stevenson's "Windy Nights," and Rudyard Kipling's "Seal Lullaby." Lighter pieces by James Thurber and Lewis Carroll are here, too. The music is for piano.

MUSIC FOR ONES AND TWOS:
SONGS AND GAMES FOR THE VERY YOUNG CHILD
by Tom Glazer
illustrated by Karen Ann Weinhaus
Doubleday, 1983

■　Glazer, one of the foremost balladeers of our time, has written short songs especially designed to appeal to babies and toddlers. And do they ever! This book includes many songs from Glazer's best-selling record, *Music for Ones and Twos* (available in many toy stores or from CMS Records, 14 Warren Street, New York, NY 10017), as well as other perennial favorites. Easy piano and guitar arrangements are included.

Board Books

BABY'S FIRST TOYS
a Teddy Board Book
Platt, 1966

■ Easy-to-recognize photographs of a ball and other toys that a baby is sure to love are set against plain colored backgrounds. Others in the series include: *Baby's First Book*; *Trucks*; *Puppies and Kittens*.

From *Max's Ride*.
Illustration by
Rosemary Wells.

MAX'S RIDE
written and illustrated by Rosemary Wells
a Very First Book
Dial, 1979

■ Max, a plump and determined rabbit, takes a wild ride in (and out of) his baby carriage, while readers explore the concepts of down, under, over, and so on. Max has great appeal to young children, particularly those with siblings, and the concepts gently introduced within the story line make the books interesting to three- and four-year-olds as well. Others in the series: *Max's First Word*; *Max's New Suit*; *Max's Toys*. Other books by Wells for two- and three-year-olds include: *Noisy Nora*; *Stanley and Rhoda*; *Timothy Goes to School*; *Unfortunately Harriet*; *Benjamin and Tulip*; *A Lion for Louis*; *Peabody*; *Abdul*; *Don't Spill It Again, James*; *Goodnight, Fred*; *Morris's Disappearing Bag: A Christmas Story*.

PLAYING
written and illustrated by Helen Oxenbury
Simon & Schuster, 1981

■ Babies can easily identify with a main character who's banging on a pot with a wooden spoon or knocking down a block tower. And parents can appreciate the funny details that Oxenbury has included. Others in the series: *Friends*; *Family*; *Dressing*; and *Working*. For graduates of the first set of books, Oxenbury provides another, with the main character now older (about 2) and able to participate in life more fully. Series titles include: *Good Night, Good Morning*; *Monkey See, Monkey Do*; *Shopping Trip*; *Mother's Helper*; *Beach Day*. (Dial)

UP THERE
written and illustrated by Eric Hill
a Baby Bear Book
Random House, 1983

■ A "see and say" book in bold colors, *Up There* features a small bear for children to identify with as he explores the world of things in the sky. Others in the series: *The Park*; *At Home*; *My Pets*. Also by Hill for slightly older children: *Where's Spot?* and its sequels.

Participation Books

DO YOU WANT TO BE MY FRIEND?
written and illustrated by Eric Carle
Crowell, 1971; Harper paperback

■ A little mouse approaches one animal at a time in search of a friend. Children can guess what animal is coming up next by looking at its tail and can then turn the page to see if they were right. Also by Carle for this age: *The Very Hungry Caterpillar*; *My Very First Book of Colors*; *My Very First Book of Numbers*; *My Very First Book of Shapes*; *My Very First Book of Words*; *One, Two, Three to the Zoo*. For three- and four-year-olds: *The Secret Birthday Message*; *The Grouchy Lady Bug*; *I See a Song*.

EACH PEACH PEAR PLUM
written and illustrated by Janet and Allan Ahlberg
Greenwillow, 1978; Scholastic paperback

■   This book stars a cast of familiar nursery rhyme characters, one of whom is hidden in each picture. The book winds up with a grand "I spy" finale, when all the characters come together to eat Mother Hubbard's pie. New details to notice with each reading. Also: *Peek-a-Boo.*

From *Each Peach Pear Plum.* Illustration by Janet and Allan Ahlberg.

FREIGHT TRAIN
written and illustrated by Donald Crews
Greenwillow, 1978

■   For twos who are passionately into transportation, *Freight Train* will be a favorite. Kids can name each of the train cars and then go on a "ride" by means of Crews's paintings, which simulate speed and motion to great effect. Other Crews books for this age: *Harbor; Carousel; Light; Truck; We Read A to Z; Ten Black Dots.*

GOBBLE GROWL GRUNT
written and illustrated by Peter Spier
Doubleday paperback, 1971

■   An enormous number of beasts — and all of them noisy — populate this book by Spier, a talented illustrator with wit and spirit. Also by the author for this age: *Crash! Bang! Boom!; Fast-Slow, High-Low.*

PAT THE BUNNY
written and illustrated by Dorothy Kunhardt
Western, 1940
- Featuring Paul and Judy, this book leads babies on a sensory exploration tour which includes stroking a furry bunny, smelling flowers, poking a finger through mother's ring, and, my personal favorite, feeling daddy's scratchy face. Kids *love* it. Also by the author in a similar style: *The Telephone Book*.

PIGS SAY OINK: A FIRST BOOK OF SOUNDS
written and illustrated by Martha Alexander
Random paperback, 1978
- City and country sounds, day and night noises, among others, are explored here. Finely detailed pictures. Also by Alexander: *Blackboard Bear* and sequels; *No Ducks in Our Bathtub*; *Maybe a Monster*; *I'll Be the Horse If You'll Play with Me*.

WHO SAID MEOW?
by Maria Polushkin
illustrated by Giulio Maestro
Crown, 1975
- Children love to follow Puppy's search for who could be saying *meow* and to find the cat peeking out on each page. Also by Polushkin for this age: *Mother, Mother, I Want Another*; *Bubba and Babba*; *The Little Hen and the Giant*; *Morning*.

First Storybooks

ASK MR. BEAR
written and illustrated by Marjorie Flack
Macmillan, 1958; Macmillan paperback
- Puzzled by what to get his mother for a birthday gift, a child asks many animals, but it is Mr. Bear who shows him the pleasures of a good bear hug. Lots of repetition, which kids like. Also by Flack for this age: *Angus*; *Angus Lost*; *Angus and the Ducks*; *Angus and the Cat*; *The Story About Ping*.

Hidden deep in a field of rye

From *Close Your Eyes*. Illustration by Susan Jeffers.

CLOSE YOUR EYES
by Jean Marzollo
illustrated by Susan Jeffers
Dial, 1978; Dial paperback

■ This lilting lullaby is accompanied by soft pictures of sleepy geese and fleecy sheep, but also by a wordless "subtext," which shows the story of a father's efforts to put his reluctant child to bed. This is a book that can be read in several different ways, depending upon the bedtime mood of you and your child. Also: *Uproar on Hollercat Hill.*

GOOD MORNING, CHICK
by Mirra Ginsburg
illustrated by Byron Barton
Greenwillow, 1980; Scholastic paperback

■ When Chick hatches, Mother Speckled Hen teaches him how to eat worms, comforts him after he falls into a pond, and hisses a cat away. Lots of animal sounds are called for here. Also: *Across the Stream; The Chick and the Duckling; Kitten from One to Ten; Mushroom in the Rain.*

FIRST BOOKS

GOODNIGHT, MOON
by Margaret Wise Brown
illustrated by Clement Hurd
Harper, 1947; Harper paperback

■ A bunny child says goodnight to all the favorite things in his room. As the bunny gets sleepier and sleepier, the illustrations grow darker and darker. Kids love to find the tiny mouse in each picture. One of Brown's most enduring works. Others to look for are: *The Little Fur Family*; *The Runaway Bunny*; *The Noisy Book*.

HARRY THE DIRTY DOG
by Gene Zion
illustrated by Margaret B. Graham
Harper, 1956; Harper paperback

■ Few children can resist the antics of Harry and his attempts to stay out of the bath. The pictures are full of energy and fun. Other Harry titles: *Harry and the Lady Next Door*; *Harry by the Sea*; *No Roses for Harry*.

I'M THE KING OF THE CASTLE
by Shigeo Watanabe
illustrated by Yasuo Ohtomo
Philomel, 1981

■ A bear plays by himself in a sandbox, builds a mountain of sand, sits on it, and becomes the "king of the castle." Subtitled as an "I Can Do It All by Myself" book, this simple story is attuned to how very young children play and reinforces the fun that can be had playing alone. Others in the series: *I Can Ride It!*; *What a Good Lunch!*; *How Do I Put It On?*; *Get Set! Go!*

MR. GUMPY'S OUTING
written and illustrated by John Burningham
Holt, 1971; Penguin paperback

■ Mr. Gumpy allows animals and children to come along on his boat ride until his little craft is so full, it tips. Mr. Gumpy never loses his sense of humor, and the book never loses its sense of fun. Sequel: *Mr.*

Gumpy's Motor Car. Also good for this age are: *The Baby*; *The Blanket*; *The Cupboard*; *The Dog*; *The Friend*; *The Rabbit*; *The School*; *The Snow.*

PLAY WITH ME
written and illustrated by Marie Hall Ets
Viking, 1955; Penguin paperback

■ An exuberant little girl invites woodland creatures to play with her, but they run away. It isn't until she sits down to rest and holds very still that they all return. Told from the little girl's point of view, the simple story and almost childlike illustrations make this a favorite with kids. Also by Ets: *In the Forest*; *Mister Penny*; *The Story of a Baby*; *Just Me.*

SAM WHO NEVER FORGETS
written and illustrated by Eve Rice
Greenwillow, 1977; Penguin paperback

■ Zookeeper Sam loads his cart with food for all the animals — except the elephant. Has he forgotten? Not a chance. Kids are reassured by the idea of a reliable Sam who won't forget them. Also by Rice for this age: *Oh, Lewis!*; *Blue Shoes.*

WHERE THE WILD THINGS ARE
written and illustrated by Maurice Sendak
Harper, 1963; Harper paperback

■ When Max wears his wolf suit and acts wild, he's sent to his room without any supper. There, he invents a fantasy in which he becomes "king of all wild things." The dreamlike quality of his adventure, the mysterious yet approachable Wild Things, and the satisfying conclusion contribute to the classic quality of this story. Also by Sendak for children two and up: *In the Night Kitchen*; *Outside Over There.* Packaged together in a tiny box, the Nutshell Library contains: *Chicken Soup with Rice*; *Pierre*; *Alligators All Around*; and *One Was Johnny.* (Sendak has a way of speaking directly to kids and putting some parents off, possibly because they feel left out. Try him and see how your child reacts and how you do.)

2
Picture Books
Ages 3 through 5

THREE-YEAR-OLDS seem to thirst for knowledge. How does the doorbell work? What makes thunder? How did I get this scar? Parents who thought themselves taxed by "Why?" from their two-year-olds are facing new, more complex questions. This is a good time to start collecting some home reference books and to begin regular trips to the library.

But a steady diet of "concept" books, books that answer questions, teach letters, numerals, colors, or different kinds of trucks or animals, is insufficient, and children who are pushed to turn reading time into "Let's see what you know" sessions often react by not wanting to read at all. At this age, it is important to foster a love of reading and to let children become emotionally involved in stories that may, as a sideline, also teach skills and concepts.

Tomie de Paola's *Charlie Needs a Cloak* is a perfect example of a book with a totally engrossing story that shows how wool is sheared from sheep, washed, carded, spun, dyed, and woven into material – to make a new cloak for Charlie, a shepherd. As the process takes place, one of Charlie's sheep seems determined to sabotage it, creating a very funny foil in the story. Children can more easily remember the information presented in this way because they have an involvement with the story to "hook" the facts on.

Threes want to know all they can about the real world, but they are also very involved in the world of make-believe, and this world needs fueling, too. This is an excellent time to introduce children to their first simple fairy tales. The best to start with are the easiest, the most repetitive, and the ones that do not involve complex motivations, such as jealousy or revenge. These tales include:

The Three Bears
The Three Billy Goats Gruff
The Three Pigs
The Gingerbread Boy (or The Pancake)
The Little Red Hen
Henny Penny
Little Red Riding Hood

Like Mother Goose rhymes, fairy tales have been time-tested by children for centuries, and they are part of our literary heritage. (It is an oddity of our era that children may first be exposed to these tales by seeing them parodied on *Sesame Street* or *Electric Company*!)

As children approach four, they may sometimes develop fears that they did not have as younger children. Witches, wolves, and people wearing masks commonly cause fright, but many children have fears with less discernible sources. It has been postulated that this is because they now understand more about the world and realize that, without adequate protection, it can be a dangerous place. It is hard to tell what triggers these fears or just what particular fears will be, so some sensitivity in the selection of reading material is advised. It is always important to preread books before reading them to children, but at this stage, this is particularly so.

Many children also have fears that can be easily understood: fear of rejection due to the birth of a new baby in the family; fear about death; fear of a trip to the doctor's office or hospital; or fear of beginning a new school. There is a plethora of books, and many good ones, which address themselves to these issues and, fortunately, many children respond enthusiastically to them. Knowing that a book character shares a fear can be comforting and can help children begin to communicate their own fears. (See References for Subject Guides to children's books.)

Compared with three- and even four-year-olds, five-year-olds seem like sophisticated citizens of the world. They can do so much for themselves and are capable of being quite independent. Yet all this worldliness can be a heavy burden for a five-year-old, and he often needs some assurance that he really *is* as capable as he sometimes believes he is. Books that have a central character who knows just how to handle things are popular with fives.

PICTURE BOOKS

The need for capable characters to identify with, as well as increased attention span for listening, make this a good time to introduce some of the more complicated fairy tales. Several Hans Christian Andersen tales and some of the less gruesome Grimm stories are appropriate. For example:

Andersen:
The Emperor's New Clothes
The Ugly Duckling
Thumbelina (or Little Tiny)

Grimm:
The Fisherman and His Wife
Rumpelstiltskin
Cinderella
Snow White and the Seven Dwarves
The Elves and the Shoemaker
Rapunzel
The Bremen Town Musicians

RECOMMENDED FAIRY TALE BOOKS

Cinderella retold by John Fowles; illustrated by Sheila Beckett; Little, Brown

Cinderella illustrated by Marcia Brown; Scribners

Deep in the Forest (a spoof of *The Three Bears*) by Brinton Turkle; Dutton

The Gingerbread Boy illustrated by Paul Galdone; Houghton

Henny Penny illustrated by Paul Galdone; Houghton

Little Red Riding Hood retold and illustrated by Trina Schart Hyman; Holiday House

Snow White and the Seven Dwarves translated and illustrated by Wanda Gag; Coward

Snow White and the Seven Dwarves translated by Randall Jarrell; illustrated by Nancy Ekholm Burkert; Farrar

The Three Billy Goats Gruff Marcia Brown; Harcourt

The Three Little Pigs illustrated by Eric Blegvad; Atheneum

The Three Wishes retold and illustrated by Paul Galdone; McGraw

The Ugly Duckling illustrated by Adrienne Adams; Scribners

PICTURE BOOKS

As you select the tales, be sure to choose versions that maintain some of the fiber and flow of the original language and, even though they may be shortened for young children, are not "sweetened" at the end. At about age five, children are ready to listen to tales with few or no illustrations, which give their imaginations free reign.

Although three-, four-, and five-year-olds are very different, the basic requirements for their books are not all that dissimilar. Some points to consider are:

- Children still love to be involved in the stories they hear. Is there an opportunity for them to chime in with different characters' voices? Sing? Pantomime? Join in on a refrain? Act out the story after it is over?

- Repetition is quite popular with this age group. Check to make sure that the language is memorable and that the amount of repetition is something that you can live with reading after reading.

- Although the text must be short enough to hold your child's attention, a variety of short and longer books is good for pacing and for increasing the ability to listen.

- Provide a variety of illustration styles and photographs for your child to look at. More stylized art as well as realistic is appropriate now, muted colors as well as brilliant ones. Don't forget to include striking black-and-white artwork in the books you select.

- Paper-engineering and pop-up books are popular with this age. Don't worry about rips and tears: they are inevitable. Have a roll of clear tape handy to reattach flaps that are torn away in the enthusiasm of the moment.

- Wordless books can be fun, particularly if your child and you like to make up stories. Be sure that the pictures are ones that really evoke a story.

- Books with spare texts that children quickly memorize are sastifying because a child gets a feeling for "reading."

- Kids like books that pose a visual riddle that can be checked by turning a page.

- Funny books are requested time and time again.

Good Books for Threes

COME TO THE DOCTOR, HARRY
written and illustrated by Mary Chalmers
Harper, 1981; Harper paperback

■   When Harry, a young cat, hurts his tail, he is taken to the doctor to have it examined and treated. A reassuring story for those who may fear doctor visits. Chalmers's books deal with real things that concern small children. The books are small and fit nicely into little hands. Also by Chalmers: *Be Good, Harry*; *Merry Christmas, Harry*; *Take a Nap, Harry*; *Throw a Kiss, Harry*.

CAPS FOR SALE
written and illustrated by Esphyr Slobodkina
Addison, 1947; Scholastic paperback

■   Children can't help but be absorbed by this story of a peddler and the monkeys that steal his caps. Memorable pictures tell the tale even without the words.

From *"Charlie Needs a Cloak"*. Illustration by Tomie de Paola.

"CHARLIE NEEDS A CLOAK"
written and illustrated by Tomie de Paola
Prentice, 1976; Scholastic paperback

■   A simple story of how a shepherd who needs a new cloak goes about getting one is enhanced by lively, clear pictures. Full of fun. Also by the author for threes: *The Comic Adventures of Old Mother Hubbard and Her Dog*; *Strega Nona*; for four and up: *The Quicksand Book*; *The Cloud Book*; *The Popcorn Book*; *Sing, Pierrot, Sing*.

CORDUROY
written and illustrated by Don Freeman
Viking, 1968; Penguin paperback

■ Corduroy is a lonely department store teddy bear until a little girl, who can see his worth beyond his missing button, comes to take him home. The story ends with a hug. Also by Freeman for this age: *A Pocket for Corduroy*; *A Rainbow of My Own*; for four and up: *Norman the Doorman*; *Hattie the Backstage Bat*.

COWBOY SMALL
written and illustrated by Lois Lenski
McKay, 1949

■ Here are a couple of days in the life of Cowboy Small, who takes good care of his horse, participates in a round-up, eats from a chuck wagon, falls off a bucking bronco, but gets up to ride again! One of Lenski's best "Small" books, which are much loved by three-year-olds. Other titles include: *The Big Book of Mr. Small*; *More Mr. Small*; *The Little Sailboat*; *The Little Farm*; *The Little Auto*; *The Little Train*; *The Little Fireman*; *The Little Airplane*.

FATHER FOX'S PENNYRHYMES
by Clyde Watson
illustrated by Wendy Watson
Crowell, 1971; Scholastic paperback

■ Kids love to chime in with the rhyming words in Watson's wonderfully fresh and terribly silly verses. The artwork is as lively as the poems, with much of it in comic strip format, telling the story in yet another way. A unique book for kids and adults. Also by the Watsons: *Hickory Stick Rag*; *Midnight Moon*; *Tom Fox and the Apple Pie*; *Applebet: An ABC*; *Fisherman's Lullabies*; *Catch Me & Kiss Me & Say It Again*.

PICTURE BOOKS

THE FORGETFUL BEARS
written and illustrated by Lawrence Weinberg
Houghton, 1982; Scholastic paperback

■ Bears so absentminded that they forget where their front door is and walk into a closet — and forget to come out — are the stars of this funny story. Kids can't help but feel more capable than this family of furry forgetters! Also: *The Forgetfuls Give a Wedding*.

MADELINE
written and illustrated by Ludwig Bemelmans
Viking, 1939; Penguin paperback

■ Here is the classic tale of the spirited Madeline and her eleven boarding-school cohorts. The language of the text is so memorable, you'll find yourself reciting it after a reading or two. Madeline is a fine heroine. Others in the series are: *Madeline's Rescue*; *Madeline and the Bad Hat*; *Madeline and the Gypsies*; *Madeline in London*.

ROSIE'S WALK
written and illustrated by Pat Hutchins
Macmillan, 1968; Macmillan paperback

■ Rosie, a barnyard hen, walks placidly along, unaware that just about to pounce on her is a fox. Pounce he does, time and time again, but as fate would have it, he always just misses the oblivious Rosie. Children find this escapade hilariously funny. Others by Hutchins for this age are: *Good Night, Owl!*; *The Wind Blew*; *The Surprise Party*; *Tom and Sam*; *Changes, Changes*; *Don't Forget the Bacon*; *Happy Birthday, Sam*.

THE TALE OF PETER RABBIT
written and illustrated by Beatrix Potter
Warne, 1903; Dover paperback

■ Flopsy, Mopsy, and Cottontail are good little bunnies, but it is the naughty Peter whom we remember. Potter's fine watercolors and her exact, descriptive prose make this book a treasure. Not all Beatrix Potter books are simple enough for three-year-olds to follow, but these are: *The Tale of Mr. Jeremy Fisher*; *The Tale of Tom Kitten*; *The Story of Miss Moppet*; *Cecily Parsley's Nursery Rhymes*.

PICTURE BOOKS

THE TEDDY BEARS' PICNIC
by Jimmy Kennedy
illustrated by Alexandra Day
Green Tiger Press, 1983; Merrimack paperback
- The old song of the bears' frolic in the woods is enchantingly and mysteriously illustrated by Day in a beautiful book, which includes a 33⅓ RPM record of the song by Bing Crosby and, on the flip side, by the Bearcats.

Good Books for Fours

ANNO'S JOURNEY
by Mitsumasa Anno
Collins, 1977
- Anno traveled from his native Japan to Europe, and this special book is a compilation of the observations, sketches, and paintings he made there. The wordless story begins with Anno arriving by boat, buying a horse, and traveling throughout the continent. The fabulously detailed pictures give readers hours of pleasure and surprises on every page, such as spying Little Red Riding Hood or following the travels of a lost balloon. A visual feast. Others by Anno include: *Anno's Counting Book*; *Anno's Alphabet*; *Anno's Counting House*; *Anno's Animals*; *Anno's Italy*; *Anno's Britain*.

BLUEBERRIES FOR SAL
written and illustrated by Robert McCloskey
Viking, 1948; Penguin paperback
- Little Sal and her mother aren't the only ones gathering food for the winter on the side of the mountain. Little Bear and his mother are there, too. As they get absorbed in their berry picking, the children wander off behind the wrong mothers! Children love the *plink!* of the berries as they hit the bottom of Sal's little tin pail, which somehow never manages to get very full. Also: *Make Way for Ducklings*; *One Morning in Maine*; *Burt Dow, Deep-Water Man*; *Lentil*.

THE BOY WHO WAS FOLLOWED HOME
by Margaret Mahy
illustrated by Steven Kellogg
Dial, 1975; Dial paperback

■ Coming home from school one day, Robert finds that he has been followed home by a hippo. Everyone in Robert's family behaves in a most civilized manner as the number of hippos increases each day, until finally it really becomes too much, and an unusual witch is called in to get rid of the beasts. Full of droll humor. Also by Mahy: *The Man Whose Mother Was a Pirate*; *The Witch in the Cherry Tree*.

CURIOUS GEORGE
written and illustrated by H. A. Rey
Houghton Mifflin, 1941; Houghton paperback

■ George is a little monkey with just one fault: he is too curious. Children can easily identify with George and the problems he causes himself because he just *has* to know. A story hour favorite. Also: *Curious George Takes a Job*; *Curious George Gets a Medal*; *Curious George Rides a Bike*; *Curious George Learns the Alphabet*; *Curious George Goes to the Hospital*.

LITTLE GORILLA
written and illustrated by Ruth Bornstein
Seabury, 1976; Scholastic paperback

■ All the jungle animals love Little Gorilla and, when he begins to grow into Big Gorilla, everyone loves him still and they show it by helping him celebrate his birthday. A deceptively simple story about the nature of love. Also: *The Dancing Man*; *The Dream of the Little Elephant*; *Jim*; *Of Course a Goat*.

MILLIONS OF CATS
written and illustrated by Wanda Gag
Coward, 1928; Coward paperback

■ When a little old man goes off in search of one cat for his wife, he finds many millions of cats! The text provides repetition at its finest and the story has a very satisfying outcome. The hand-lettering in this masterful black-and-white book blends exquisitely with the illustrations. Also by Gag: *The Funny Thing*; *Snippy and Snappy*; *The ABC Bunny*; *Gone Is Gone*; *Nothing at All*. For older children: *Tales from Grimm*.

From
Millions of Cats.
Illustration by
Wanda Gag.

And they began to quarrel.

MOONLIGHT
written and illustrated by Jan Ormerod
Lothrop, 1982; Morrow paperback
■   A wordless wonder of a book about a little girl's bedtime in sequences that portray a real family's routine, clutter, and tiredness at the end of day. An original way of touching upon the familiar nighttime scene. A companion book about getting up in the morning: *Sunshine*.

PETER'S CHAIR
written and illustrated by Ezra Jack Keats
Harper, 1967; Harper paperback
■   When Peter sees all his baby things being freshly painted for his new sister, he quickly rescues his little chair, only to find that he can no longer fit into it. On his own, he decides how to handle a difficult situation. Keats has illustrated the book with collage, which is lovely, effective, and at times, amusing. Also by Keats for this age: *The Snowy Day*; *Whistle for Willie*; *Goggles*; *Hi, Cat!*; *The Little Drummer Boy*; *Louie*; *Pet Show!*; *The Trip*.

Good Books for Fives

BEA AND MR. JONES
written and illustrated by Amy Schwartz
Bradbury, 1983; Penguin paperback

- Bea is sick of kindergarten and her father, Mr. Jones, is tired of the same old routine at the office. And so they trade places, with great success and happiness for each. The new-wave art is perfect for the tongue-in-cheek humor of the text.

From *Bea and Mr. Jones*.
Illustration by
Amy Schwartz.

BEDTIME FOR FRANCES
by Russell Hoban
illustrated by Garth Williams
Harper, 1960; Harper paperback

- Frances, a badger-child, can't sleep, and she uses every trick in the book to involve her understanding-up-to-a-point parents in her dilemma. Hoban has perfectly captured a five-year-old in Frances. Sequels: *A Baby Sister for Frances*; *A Birthday for Frances*; *A Bargain for Frances*; *Best Friends for Frances*; *Bread and Jam for Frances*; *Egg Thoughts and Other Frances Songs*.

THE CARROT SEED
by Ruth Krauss
illustrated by Crockett Johnson
Harper, 1945; Scholastic paperback

■ A simple, memorable story of a boy who tends his carrot seed even though everyone in his family keeps telling him "It won't come up." In the end, persistence is rewarded and the little guy proves, once again, to have been wiser than the big guys. Also by Kraus: *Bears*; *The Happy Egg*; *I'll Be You — You Be Me*; *Monkey Day*; *Somebody Else's Nut Tree*; *A Hole Is to Dig*; *Is This You?*

THE CHURCH MICE AND THE MOON
written and illustrated by Graham Oakley
Atheneum, 1974; Atheneum paperback

■ In this zany pseudospace adventure, a group of mice and a helpful feline named Samson outsmart some overambitious lunar scientists. A very funny text and irreverent illustrations make the Church Mice books favorites with five-year-old boys particularly. Others in the series: *The Church Cat Abroad*, *The Church Mice Adrift*, *The Church Mice Spread Their Wings*, *The Church Mice at Bay*, and *The Church Mice at Christmas*.

From
*The Church Mice
and the Moon*.
Illustration by
Graham Oakley.

CROW BOY
written and illustrated by Taro Yashima
Viking, 1955; Penguin paperback

■ A small boy's fear and loneliness at a new school are remarkably evoked by Yashima's crayon drawings. A sensitive teacher finds the boy's special talent — imitating the different sounds of crows — and helps him share it with his classmates. Also by Yashima: *Umbrella*; *The Village Tree*.

FREDERICK
written and illustrated by Leo Lionni
Pantheon, 1966; Pantheon paperback

■ As his mouse family gathers food for the coming winter, Frederick just sits there. He is gathering images and stories to feed the spirits of the mice during their hibernation. One of the most superlative definitions of an artist/poet ever. Others by Lionni: *Swimmy*; *Little Blue and Little Yellow*; *Alexander and the Wind-up Mouse*; *Fish Is Fish*.

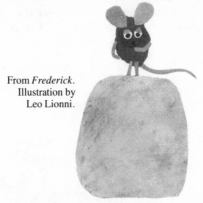

From *Frederick*.
Illustration by
Leo Lionni.

LITTLE TIM AND THE BRAVE SEA CAPTAIN
written and illustrated by Edward Ardizzoni
Oxford, 1955; Penguin paperback

■ Tim runs away to sail the seas, and after surviving hardships and adventures, returns home again, a hero. Children love the vicarious thrills and shouldn't miss Ardizzoni's incredible drawings. Others by

Ardizzoni: *Lucy Brown and Mr. Grimes*; *Tim in Danger*; *Ship's Cook Ginger*; *Tim and Ginger*; *Tim All Alone*; *Tim and Charlotte*; *Tim's Friend Towser*; *Tim's Last Voyage*; *Tim to the Lighthouse*.

THE SIGN ON ROSIE'S DOOR
written and illustrated by Maurice Sendak
Harper, 1960; Harper paperback
■ Four short stories about Rosie and her gang of friends dressing up, putting on plays that never quite get going, and inventing imaginary games. The sense of real children at play is very strong. Also by Sendak for this age: *Kenny's Window*; *Very Far Away*; *Higgledy Piggledy Pop!*

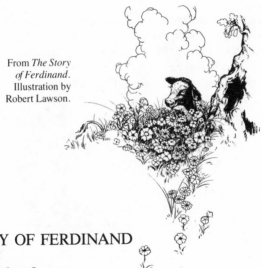

From *The Story of Ferdinand*. Illustration by Robert Lawson.

THE STORY OF FERDINAND
by Munro Leaf
illustrated by Robert Lawson
Viking, 1936; Penguin paperback
■ Ferdinand the bull does not run and butt his horns with the other little bulls, but prefers to sit quietly and smell the flowers. The fine-tuned story of Ferdinand's near-brush with bull fighting and Lawson's expressive black-and-white illustrations make this a not-to-be-missed classic. Ferdinand is a peace-loving individualist, an inspiration to us all. Also by Leaf: *Noodle*; *Who Cares? I Do!*

PICTURE BOOKS

The tenth good thing about Barney
by Judith Viorst
illustrated by Eric Blegvad
Atheneum, 1975; Atheneum paperback

■ "My cat Barney died last Friday. I was very sad." So begins Viorst's sterling picture book about life, death, and remembering. A better introduction to the subject would be hard to find. Also by Viorst: *Alexander and the Terrible, Horrible, No Good, Very Bad Day*; *Alexander Who Used to Be Rich Last Sunday*; *I'll Fix Anthony*; *Sunday Morning*.

Tell me a Mitzi
by Lore Segal
illustrated by Harriet Pincus
Farrar, 1970; Scholastic paperback

■ Three short stories telling, in excruciating detail which kids relish, stories of Martha and her little brother Jacob. Pincus's illustrations seem to move along with the story. They're full-bodied and so satisfying.

From *Tell Me A Mitzi*.
Illustration by Harriet Pincus.

When I was young in the mountains
by Cynthia Rylant
illustrated by Diane Goode
Dutton, 1983

■ Overflowing with love of mountain life and rich in details of okra, corn bread, swimming holes, porch swings, and church in the schoolhouse on Sundays, this book evokes warm feelings for a simple, good way of life.

3
Books for Beginning Readers
Ages 6 through 8

SOME TIME AROUND THE AGE OF SIX or so, most children proudly proclaim, "I can read!" It often does seem to happen almost overnight that a child who was able to manage only single words can suddenly read whole sentences. But reading is something like playing tennis: When can you truly play tennis? When you can hit the ball over the net? Master a backhand? Return a serve? Keep score? Win a tournament? It's a gradual process that takes time and practice to perfect.

Probably no skill will be more important than reading in determining a child's future success in school, and possibly in major life choices. So it's no surprise that reading is the number one learning priority of both children and parents during the early elementary school years. Often, an hour or more out of a school day is devoted to the teaching of reading as a separate subject from first through sixth grade, and beyond that in many junior highs. Yet even with the considerable time and effort given to reading in our schools, the scores of children on standardized reading tests are pretty dismal. Beginning readers from six to eight must not only master basic reading skills, such as sounding out unfamiliar words or determining the meaning of an unknown word from context, but they need to be motivated to *want* to learn to read. This is the key: kids need to understand that learning to read is going to pay off.

A child who has been read good books since cradle days knows that learning to read independently will give her access to more of the wonderful stories that she already loves. A child who has spent her preschool years playing in the sandbox or watching TV but has not had books as a part of her life will need some help in understanding why learning to read is so important.

Probably the best way you can help a beginning reader, whether she is already book-hooked or not, is to continue to read good books aloud to her, even after she "officially" knows how to read herself. Jim Trelease, author of the bestselling *Read-Aloud Handbook*, makes a strong case for the near-miracles that reading aloud can do for reluctant readers, and he offers hundreds of suggestions for good books to read aloud.

The child who is just beginning to read may recognize only a limited number of words on the printed page of her school preprimer, but her listening vocabulary is far more advanced. This is a good time to read aloud stories with vivid, precise words and flowing sentences to provide a contrast to the repetitious words and staccato sentences of the school texts. Picture books that have quite a bit of text compared to earlier picture books are a good place to begin reading. From these books, you can move to books with fewer and fewer pictures, and then to short novels with chapters that can be read during a brief reading time each day.

In addition to contemporary picture books and novels, listening to fairy tales can be a rewarding experience. The language of these tales is rich and evocative, having been honed by centuries of oral tradition. And the themes of the tales, according to eminent child psychologist Bruno Bettelheim, can help children deal with the larger questions they may have about life, but are unable to express adequately, such as: Who am I? What kind of person will I be when I grow up? What does life mean? In his masterful book on the subject, *The Uses of Enchantment*, Bettelheim stresses that fairy tales speak to children on a preconscious level and can help them understand and cope with the struggles that one inevitably faces in life.

Think how many fairy tales involve a character, often the youngest brother, who people do not think can accomplish much. Though he meets great obstacles in life, he emerges victorious, often gaining a kingdom and the respect of those who had laughed at him. How satisfying for a child who feels so like this youngest child (no matter where her actual place in the family constellation may be) to identify with such a hero and to learn that seemingly impossible trials in life can, through persistence and kindness, often be overcome. Unlike myths, which can have tragic endings, or fables, which are thinly disguised lessons, fairy tales always end happily, giving something vital to young listeners: hope.

BOOKS FOR BEGINNING READERS

At about age six or seven, when they begin to understand the difference between reality and fantasy, children are usually ready for some of the more sophisticated fairy tales. Of course prereading and discretion are necessary to find a tale both you and your child will enjoy. Bettelheim believes that telling the tales rather than reading them is best. As you tell a tale to your child, your sensitivity to her and to her hopes and fears of the moment can lead you to expand some aspects of the story and play down others, while still being faithful to the story itself. The slight alterations you make, both consciously and unconsciously, will give a fairy tale your own personal flavor, and will increase its significance to your child.

Another good way to motivate a beginning reader besides reading aloud is to provide her with good books that she can read all by herself. For a new reader, nothing is more satisfying than reading a whole book solo. Most publishers have series of books intended to be read by children in the first and second grades who are just beginning to read. The series have different titles, such as Beginner Books or Let Me Read, all connoting early independent reading, and they all have several things in common:

- They are quite slim—and unintimidating.
- They have fairly large type.
- There may be a lot of white space between lines of type.
- They use short sentences.
- They are based on a "controlled vocabulary." That is, for the most part they use words from a list of very easy words likely to be familiar to beginning readers.
- There is usually an illustration on every page, but the character of the pictures is more sophisticated than that of picture books, and the illustrations often give visual clues that will help a beginning reader comprehend the story.
- A reading level may be given just inside the front cover, on the copyright page, or on the back cover. A level of 2.5, for example, would be what an average reader in the fifth month of second grade could handle. Reading levels are a good guide, but shouldn't be taken as law.
- The best of these books have language that sounds natural and conversational, not choppy and forced. Repetition of certain words and phrases can help a new reader gain confidence.

BOOKS FOR BEGINNING READERS

Kids usually aren't in the controlled vocabulary books for very long, but for that time, these books can play a vital role in motivating kids to read. Reading these books aloud can be helpful to a child who's just learning to decode, but be sure to balance these readings with more challenging books.

As children make the transition from controlled vocabulary books to storybooks, the first books they choose have much in common with the easy-readers: they are slim, heavily illustrated, many are paperback, and the type is still fairly big. But the sentences are longer and the vocabulary is not limited. From these books, kids can move into books that are considered early novels. Some things to consider when helping an early reader choose books are:

- At first, there should be just one story line; subplots tend to be confusing.
- Kids like tension in their stories: lots of narrow escapes and near-misses. They experience a great sense of relief in satisfying, happy endings. Unhappy endings can still be very upsetting to a child at this stage.
- Kids like to read fiction about things they are experiencing in their own lives: families and how they get along, school stories, feeling lonely, and so on.
- Kids at this age also like exotic settings and fantasy and are beginning to have an appreciation for the past.

Kids from six through eight like to select their own books, and this can be a tremendous boost to motivation. They are well aware of what their friends are reading, what's in and what's not. They may want to order their own books from a book club offered through their school each month. School book clubs offer paperbacks, popular with kids and usually sold for less than the price of bookstore books. (They are actually less expensive editions, printed on cheaper paper, but are a bargain considering their low cost.) In a given month, selections usually include books about TV shows or movies, jokes and riddles, contemporary fiction, controlled vocabulary books, as well as classics. Book fairs, organized by schools in conjunction with publishers, are also a popular way for children to pick out their own good books.

Good Books
For Reading Aloud

PICTURE BOOKS

DOCTOR DESOTO
written and illustrated by William Steig
Farrar, 1982

■ Wisely, Dr. Desoto, a mouse and a dentist, refuses to work on the teeth of animals that like mice — for dinner. But one day he takes pity on a fox with a rotten bicuspid, and he is forced to call up all of his resourcefulness to keep from being eaten. Steig's precise prose and his tremendous sense of fun make this book a joy to read. Also by Steig for this age: *Amos and Boris*; *The Amazing Bone*; *Farmer Palmer's Wagon Ride*; *Caleb and Kate.*

From
Doctor Desoto.
Illustration by
William Steig.

THE GARDEN OF ABDUL GASAZI
written and illustrated by Chris Van Allsburg
Houghton, 1979

■ When a strong-willed dog runs away into a retired magician's garden where a sign on the gate says, "Absolutely, Positively No Dogs Allowed," Alan reluctantly follows him in to where the real and unreal meet. The haunting, beautiful illustrations and the nice surprises at the end make this book a satisfying one. Also by the author: *Ben's Dream*; *Jumanji.*

BOOKS FOR BEGINNING READERS

GILA MONSTERS MEET YOU AT THE AIRPORT
by Marjorie Weinman Sharmat
illustrated by Byron Barton
Macmillan, 1980

- A New York City boy dreads his family's move "Out West" because of his very funny stereotyped ideas of what it's like out there. A wonderful book for talking about prejudice and about moving — or to read just for fun.

From *Gila Monsters
Meet You at the Airport*.
Illustration by
Byron Barton.

IRA SLEEPS OVER
written and illustrated by Bernard Waber
Houghton, 1972; Houghton paperback

- The dilemma of whether Ira should bring his teddy bear with him when he sleeps over at a friend's house is explored with much warmth and wit. Also by Waber: *Lyle, Lyle, Crocodile*; *Lovable Lyle*; *Lyle and the Birthday Party*; *Lyle Finds His Mother*.

MISS RUMPHIUS
written and illustrated by Barbara Cooney
Viking, 1982

- Alice's grandfather tells her that she needs to find a way — her own way — to make the world more beautiful. She chooses to sow seeds of lupine, a tall blue flower, all over the landscape. As an old woman, she is known as the "lupine lady" and she passes on her grandfather's words to other children. A book with a marvelous feeling for the cycles of life: times for sowing, times for reaping. The illustrations are breathtakingly beautiful. Also: *Christmas*.

WHERE BUFFALOES BEGIN
by Olaf Baker
illustrated by Stephen Gammell
Warne, 1981

■　An authentic adventure story with evocative black-and-white drawings, in which Little Wolf, age ten, finds the legendary lake from which buffaloes rise to the earth. The prairie is soon the stage for a wild stampede, with Little Wolf in the lead to save his people.

For Reading Aloud

NOVELS

THE BEST CHRISTMAS PAGEANT EVER
by Barbara Robinson
Harper, 1972; Avon paperback

■　A humorous book about a Sunday school pageant which is taken over by the toughest kids in town.

CHARLOTTE'S WEB
by E. B. White
illustrated by Garth Williams
Harper, 1952; Dell paperback

■　For beautiful, clear prose style, it is hard to top *Charlotte's Web*, the tender story of Wilbur, a runt pig, and his friendship with a wise and inventive spider named Charlotte. A favorite with children and adults alike, the story's universal theme of life and death makes it a memorable classic. Also by E. B. White: *Stuart Little*; *The Trumpet of the Swan*.

THE CHOCOLATE TOUCH
by Patrick Skene Catling
Morrow, 1979; Bantam paperback

■　A variation on the Midas story that chocolate-loving children will find amusing.

BOOKS FOR BEGINNING READERS

JAMES AND THE GIANT PEACH
by Roald Dahl
illustrated by Nancy Ekholm Burkert
Knopf, 1961; Bantam paperback

■   When two crotchety aunts take in the orphaned James, it seems that
life will only offer drudgery, until one day when a giant peach shows
up in James's yard and whisks him away. Also by Dahl: *The Magic
Finger; Fantastic Mr. Fox; Danny the Champion of the World; The
Wonderful Story of Henry Sugar; The Enormous Crocodile; George's
Marvelous Medicine.*

From *James and the Giant Peach*.
Illustration by Nancy Ekholm Burkert.

MY FATHER'S DRAGON
by Ruth S. Gannett
illustrated by Ruth S. Gannett
Random House, 1948; Dell paperback

■   A small boy ventures forth to save a baby dragon from an island in-
habited by cruel animals who have him tied up. Luckily, he packs useful things in his pack and uses them with great facility to accomplish
his mission. Intriguing, but not scary. Sequels: *Elmer and the Dragon;
The Dragons of Blueland.*

PIPPI LONGSTOCKING
by Astrid Lindgrin
illustrated by Louis S. Glanzman
Viking, 1950; Penguin paperback

■   Pippi lives the life that every child, at some time or another, wishes she
led: she can make an enormous mess in the kitchen without getting a

scolding, she keeps a horse on her front porch, and she doesn't have to go to school. Kids alternately envy her and worry over her parentless plight. Also in the series: *Pippi Goes on Board*; *Pippi in the South Seas*. Picture books by Lindgrin suitable for this age group: *The Tomten*; *The Tomten and the Fox*.

Winnie the Pooh
by A. A. Milne
illustrated by Ernest Shepard
Dutton, 1926; Dell paperback

■ Young Christopher Robin's stuffed bear, donkey, pig, kangaroo, and rabbit have become immortalized in this classic childhood story. Shepard's illustrations endow Pooh and company with just what Mr. Milne must have had in mind as he wrote. Also: *The House at Pooh Corner*; and two volumes of not-to-be-missed poetry, *When We Were Very Young* and *Now We Are Six*.

For Reading Aloud

FAIRY TALE COLLECTIONS

The Arthur Rackham Fairy Book
illustrated by Arthur Rackham
Lippincott, 1950

■ Rackham's illustrations have true gothic fairy-tale quality. This edition is for the more mature listeners in this age category.

The Fairy Tale Treasury
compiled by Virginia Haviland
illustrated by Raymond Briggs
Coward, 1980

■ A sturdy collection selected by an authority in the field of children's literature.

BOOKS FOR BEGINNING READERS

THE JUNIPER TREE
by the Brothers Grimm
illustrated by Maurice Sendak
Farrar, 1973; Dell paperback
- Two volumes of tales with haunting illustrations by Sendak.

THE PROVENSEN BOOK OF FAIRY TALES
compiled and illustrated by Alice and Martin Provensen
Random House, 1971
- The Provensens provide a masterful interpretation of the classic tales.

THE RAINBOW FAIRY BOOK
collected by Arthur Lang
edited by Kathleen Lines
illustrated by Margery Gill
Schocken Books, 1977
- For reading aloud or as a source of tales for telling, Lang's authoritative "Color Fairy Books" are hard to beat.

TALES FROM GRIMM
freely translated and illustrated by Wanda Gag
Coward, 1936; Coward paperback
- Gag explains in her introduction that she went for the spirit of the tale and was not slavish about the literal text. The results are wonderful, and Gag's spirited illustrations in black-and-white add to the fun.

THE THREE BEARS AND FIFTEEN OTHER STORIES
by Anne Rockwell
Crowell, 1975
- This collection includes the "beast tales," suitable for the younger children in this age category, as well as other simple tales.

WOMANFOLK AND FAIRY TALES
by Rosemary Minard
Houghton, 1975
- For those who complain that women are seldom the central figures in fairy tales, here's the perfect collection.

For Independent Reading

CONTROLLED VOCABULARY BOOKS

FOX AT SCHOOL
by Edward Marshall
illustrated by James Marshall
Dial "Easy-to-Read," 1983; Dial paperback

■ A class play, a fire drill, and a teacher leaving the classroom for a moment are the situations for three short stories in which Fox, a lovable goof-off, has his hilarious ups and downs. Reading level: 2.0. Other Easy-to-Reads by Marshall: *Fox and His Friends*; *Fox in Love*; *Fox on Wheels*; *Three by the Sea*.

From *Fox at School*.
Illustration by
James Marshall.

LITTLE BEAR
by Else Minarik
illustrated by Maurice Sendak
Harper "I Can Read," 1957; Harper paperback

■ Little Bear's antics and his mother's good-natured understanding make this a story that any young child will love. Sendak's Little Bear is one of the most lovable characters ever pictured. Others in the series: *Father Bear Comes Home*; *Little Bear's Friend*; *Little Bear's Visit*; *A Kiss for Little Bear*. Also in "I Can Read" by Minarik and Sendak: *No Fighting, No Biting!*

BOOKS FOR BEGINNING READERS

MEET M AND M
by Pat Ross
illustrated by Marilyn Hafner
Pantheon, 1980; Dell "Yearling" paperback

■ Mandy and Mimi are such good friends they pretend to be twins until "one crabby day everything went wrong." The story gives a sense of how it feels when a friend is mad, and the good feeling of making up. Also: *M and M and the Haunted House Game.*

From *Meet M and M*.
Illustration by
Marilyn Hafner.

MOUSE TALES
written and illustrated by Arnold Lobel
Harper "I Can Read," 1972; Harper paperback

■ Papa mouse tells seven tales to his seven mouse boys at bedtime. They're all amusing and several offer some nice insights and ironies for kids to consider. Other "I Can Reads" by Lobel: *Mouse Soup*; *Frog and Toad Are Friends*; *Frog and Toad Together*; *Grasshopper on the Road*. Others by Lobel for this age group: *Ming Lo Moves the Mountain*; *Pigericks.*

NATE THE GREAT
by Marjorie Weinman Sharmat
illustrated by Marc Simont
Coward, 1972; Dell "Yearling" paperback

■ Kids love Nate, a self-proclaimed Great Detective, and they respond to Sharmat's lively humor. Also: *Nate the Great Goes Undercover*; *Nate the Great and the Sticky Case*; *Nate the Great and the Lost List*; *Nate the Great and the Phony Clue.*

From *Red Sun Girl*.
Illustration by
Susan Meddaugh.

RED SUN GIRL
by Jean and Claudio Marzollo
illustrated by Susan Meddaugh
Dial "Easy-to-Read," 1983; Dial paperback

■ On a world with two suns lives Kiri, the only being who does not take on an animal form when the Blue Sun appears. Her quest to attain an animal identity makes good reading for budding sci-fi adventure fans. Other Easy-to-Reads by Marzollo: *Amy Goes Fishing*; *Jed's Junior Space Patrol*; *Robin of Bray*.

For Independent Reading

TRANSITIONAL BOOKS

AMELIA BEDELIA
by Peggy Parish
illustrated by Fritz Siebel
Harper, 1963; Harper paperback

■ Every crop of young readers falls for the word-play zanies in the Amelia stories, which feature a befuddled maid who takes instructions literally. To dust the furniture she sprinkles it with bath powder! Luckily, she makes a great pie and manages to hold on to her job. Others: *Thank You, Amelia Bedelia*; *Amelia Bedelia and the Surprise Shower*; *Come Back, Amelia Bedelia*; *Play Ball, Amelia Bedelia*.

BOOKS FOR BEGINNING READERS

CAM JANSEN
AND THE MYSTERY OF THE DINOSAUR BONES
by David Adler
illustrated by Susanna Natti
Viking, 1981; Dell "Yearling" paperback

■ Jennifer earned her nickname Cam from her incredible photographic memory, which helps her solve mysteries. Also: *Cam Jansen and the Mystery of the U.F.O.*; *Cam Jansen and the Case of the Stolen Diamonds.*

DRACULA
by Bram Stoker
adapted by Stephanie Spinner
illustrated by Jim Spence
Random House "Step-Up Adventure," 1982

■ The old horror tale has been skillfully adapted by Spinner to retain its eerie quality yet be accessible to new readers. Others in the Step-Up series are: *King Solomon's Mines*; *Mysteries of Sherlock Holmes*; *King Kong*; *Frankenstein*; *Kon-Tiki*; *Dr. Jekyll and Mr. Hyde.*

For Independent Reading

EARLY NOVELS

FRECKLE JUICE
by Judy Blume
illustrated by Sonia Lisker
Four Winds, 1971; Dell paperback

■ Since everyone else has freckles, Andrew wants them, too, and is willing to try anything to get them, even an odd recipe for "freckle juice." Others by Blume for this age: *Tales of a Fourth Grade Nothing*; *Superfudge.*

GHOST TOWN TREASURE
by Clyde Robert Bulla
Crowell, 1958; Scholastic paperback

■ In an old frontier diary, Ty finds a clue that may lead him to a cave with a treasure of gold inside. He and his friends Nora and Paul try to find the cave as time for the treasure hunt runs out. Full of suspense and action. Others by Bulla for this age range: *The Ghost of Windy Hill*; *My Friend the Monster*; *A Ranch for Danny*; *Surprise for a Cowboy*; *Shoeshine Girl*; *Dexter*; *Marco Moonlight*.

HOW TO EAT FRIED WORMS
by Thomas Rockwell
Watts, 1973; Dell paperback
■   Two boys make a bet that one of them will eat fifteen worms in fifteen days or lose fifty dollars. The resulting situations are slightly nauseating and absolutely hilarious.

RAMONA THE PEST
by Beverly Cleary
illustrated by Louis Darling
Morrow, 1968; Dell paperback
■   Cleary really knows how to write for third graders. Her tale of Ramona's kindergarten days will evoke nostalgia and laughter from her now older and wiser audience. Also terrific Cleary reading for this age: *Ramona and Her Father*; *Ramona and Her Mother*; *Ramona Quimby, Age 8*; *Ramona the Brave*; *Beezus and Ramona*; *Henry and Beezus*; *Henry and Ribsy*; *Henry and the Paper Route*.

A TOAD FOR TUESDAY
by Russell Erickson
illustrated by Lawrence Di Fiori
Lothrop, 1974; Dell paperback
■   Warton, a big-hearted toad, sets off in the snow to take some special beetle brittle to his Aunt Toolia who lives far away. His journey is interrupted when an owl snatches him up and carries him away to his oak tree, promising to devour him five days hence, on Tuesday. But five days is long enough for a friendship to bud, and Warton gets to stick around to be in Erickson's funny and warm sequels. They are: *Warton and Morton*; *Warton and the Castaways*; *Warton and the King of the Skies*; *Warton's Christmas Eve Adventure*; *Warton and the Traders*.

4
Books for Middle Graders
Ages 9 through 11

BY FOURTH GRADE, many children have left behind the days of struggling with words of more than one syllable and are reading fluently. Their school reading instruction now consists of comprehension exercises and critical reading drills to deepen their ability to understand what they are reading.

Fourth grade can be a marvelous time for a good reader. The amount of homework he has is not usually overwhelming, nor is his schedule of after-school activities. He has time on his hands, eagerness in his heart, and a world of books at his fingertips with which to fill the hours and fuel the enthusiasm.

Fifth and sixth graders are generally more involved with their friends than are fourth graders, and they don't spend as much time reading outside of school as younger kids do, but many of them still manage to do quite a bit of reading. A good middle-grade reader usually reads a wide variety of things: mysteries, sports biographies, comic books, joke books, movie novelizations, adventure stories, and fantasies. For these kids, variety is the perfect prescription for becoming better and better readers: challenging material is needed to move them forward as strong readers and the easier material will provide practice and confidence, and will solidify the skills they have already gained. I know when I finish a very thought-provoking book, I don't want to start another one right away. I want time to digest the issues in the first one, so I prefer to read a light mystery or magazine articles for a while. Kids, too, I think, find a steady diet of challenging books a bit heavy.

In trying to vary their usual material, many good middle-grade readers will get hooked on series books for a while. It is the rare fifth grader who has not opened the cover of a Hardy Boys adventure or a Bobbsey Twins story, which are referred to as "formula fiction," because they aren't written out of an author's deep-seated desire to express himself, but by a system of fast-paced, suspenseful episodes without much character development or important thematic material. Some parents and teachers despair when their kids — especially the good readers — go on a Hardy Boys binge, for example, yet there almost seems to be in middle graders some deep inner requirement for this kind of fiction. Perhaps it's because it's so safe: the characters behave in *very* predictable ways, the heroes *always* manage to escape precarious situations, and when the story is over, it's over, with no moral dilemmas to ponder, no sorrow and no pain.

But even if your child seems to be stuck on formula fiction, take heart: I know personally several extremely literate women, readers of Proust, Dickens, and Jane Austen, whose eyes glaze over with fond memories when recalling Nancy Drew, her boyfriend Ned, and the incredible independence she had tooling around in her blue roadster. The Nancy Drew stage doesn't last forever and it doesn't prohibit a child from moving on to more hearty fare. If you want to hasten the process, try leaving a John Bellairs mystery on the kitchen table and see what happens.

In choosing good books for this age group, look for:
- a "hook" on the first couple of pages that makes a reader want to know more;
- language that communicates clearly and has a good, original, but not overbearing, style;
- characters that are fresh and believable rather than stereotyped;
- a plot that makes a reader want to keep on reading to find out what will happen next.

Some books for kids in the middle grades take on problems that many kids do have to face: divorce, death of a loved one, serious illness, alcoholism, drug abuse, battling families, runaways. For children of this age, such topics need to be handled extremely well. Simply preachy message books should be ignored. Books that end on a note of despair are not suitable for this age group either. Authors of books for middle graders have a responsibility to portray the world to developing children as a place where, despite all its serious problems, there is some hope, for an eleven-year-old is powerless to take measures to improve problematic situations.

BOOKS FOR MIDDLE GRADERS

A word about censorship seems appropriate for this age group because of the subject matter of some of the books. Many sixth graders are already reading what are known as "young adult" books, which go even farther into subjects, such as sex or drugs, or which contain language that you may feel uncomfortable about having your child read. If you are considering forbidding your child to read a certain book that he has expressed interest in, you might want to take the following steps:

1. Read the book yourself. Consider whether the topics that concern you are there just to spice up a dull story or whether they are an integral part of a meaningful story, intended to show motivation for a certain action or character development. Consider how the issues in the book are handled. If shoplifting is dealt with, for example, it shouldn't be glamorized or rewarded in the end.

2. Consider whether the topics involved might actually be helpful for your child to read about and for the two of you to discuss afterwards. For example, a good book about peer pressure to use drugs might not only help your child to think about the problem, but might also be a vicarious experience that would save him from learning a hard lesson from firsthand experience. And talking about characters in a book and *their* problems can be a lot easier than talking to your own child about *his* problems.

3. If you feel that the book is not worthy of your child's reading or that the subject matter and the way it is handled might be disturbing to him, talk about this with your child and let him know how you feel. Listen to his side, too. Perhaps the two of you could search for another book that deals with the same topic in a way that is acceptable to both of you. Be aware that absolutely prohibiting a book to a child in this age group may lead only to a secret reading of it anyway, and may lose you an opportunity to interact with him about something very important.

4. If you feel that the story is good enough for your child to read, despite the four-letter words or controversial topics, you might want to follow up by comparing your reactions with his after he has read it. If handled in a low-key way, such books can lead to communication and shared experiences at a time when many parents and children are beginning to find it difficult to relate to each other.

Motivating Middle-Grade Readers:

So far, this chapter has dealt with the good or at least average readers in the middle grades. But at the other end of the spectrum are the kids who are still baffled by *The Cat in the Hat*; the kids who watch even more TV than the average of twenty-five hours each week that has been tabulated for middle-grade kids; the ones who would rather play video games or touch football than read; the ones who, when a book report is due, scan the library shelves for the book with the very skinniest spine. These are the poor readers and the uninterested readers, the ones who are turned off reading. Many librarians I spoke to while researching this book told me that most of the parents they speak to wanted desperately to know about books for kids who weren't interested in reading. And so, the rest of this chapter is devoted to suggestions for motivating middle-grade kids to read — and like it!

- *Keep reading aloud*, whether your child is still having difficulty with reading or is a competent reader. No one ever outgrows the pleasure of hearing a good story read out loud. Betsy Hearne, author of *Choosing Books for Children*, gives an excellent suggestion: read aloud the first chapter of a new book to your child. This way, he'll want to find out what happens, and will finish the book on his own.

- *Compete with TV.* TV shows that kids like are usually full of action and suspense that fit neatly into seven-minute segments between commercials. Kids who are TV addicts have no patience for books that take a chapter or two to get going. Try some short and snappy books like the Pick-a-Path™ or Twist-a-Plot™ series (Scholastic) or the Choose Your Own™ Adventure books (Bantam). These books feature the reader as the main character, immediately involving kids. The stories are fast-moving, quickly coming to a point where a vital decision must be made and *you*, the reader, make it. If, for example, you think you should follow a sneaky-looking guy in a trench coat, you are directed to turn to a certain page to continue that story. But if you think you should follow the little green alien instead, you are directed to another page to continue along that plot line, until another decision needs to be made.

- *Use TV and movie tie-ins.* If your child is fascinated by a program on the unusual animals of Australia, see if you can help him find a book about them that will tell him more. (See pg. 12 for an explanation of how *The Subject Guide to Children's Books in Print* can help you with this.) If a new movie has captured his attention, check at a bookstore to see if there's a book by the same title. TV movies, as well as feature films, are frequently adapted from books.

- *Go for the big laugh.* It's hard for even the most resistant reader to say no to a book that's really hilarious. Try some by Jane and Jovial Bob Stine, known to most middle graders as editors of the popular *Dynamite* and *Bananas* magazines. The Stines' *Don't Step in the Soup* is a spoof on an etiquette guide. For boys, the section on how to dress correctly advises: "Stay away from stores that sell both men's suits and live bait."

- *Cater to the comic book buff* by supplying him with a *Tin Tin* (pronounced *tan-tan*) or *Asterix* adventure. These large-format ultracomics have speech balloons and plenty of *biff!* and *splosh!*, but they're quite sophisticated in their story lines as well as in their wit. And since they're quite lengthy, they give kids practice in concentration.

- *Let your child pick out his own books.* By the middle grades, most kids know just what they want to read, and choosing their own books is big motivation for reading. School book clubs are very popular with kids in the middle grades, and the books' prices are quite affordable. Some bookstores have special charge accounts for middle-grade kids. Parents deposit a certain amount to the account a couple of times a year, and kids feel very independent being able to get their books solo. Libraries, too, are on to the fact that kids want paperbacks, and they have them, often in bookstore-like carousels that kids like to investigate.

- *Take advantage of peer pressure.* Kids are quick to recommend good books to each other, and fad reading isn't necessarily bad reading. (Several fifth-grade girls I spoke to told me that the hot book in their class this year was *Anne of Green Gables* — a classic first published in 1908!) Your child's teacher, school librarian, or best friend may be able to clue you in on what everyone's reading this semester so that you can encourage your child to read it, too.

- *But . . . be temperate in the books you recommend.* At this stage, enthusiastic adult approval of a book is usually its death knell. Be casual.

- *Go with a child's interests.* When kids care passionately about a subject, they'll often read material on it that is way above their normal comprehension level because they are so motivated. Girls in sixth grade who seem interested only in designer jeans and who was seen talking to whom at the drinking fountain will probably like reading the romance series such as Wildfire (Scholastic), First Love (Pocket Books), and Sweet Dreams (Bantam), which are written especially for the younger romantics and don't have much explicit action — just lots of wishful anticipation. Most of these books are pretty formulized — in fact, there is a list of specific guidelines sent to would-be romance writers detailing the do's and don'ts of the genre — but at least a romance reader is reading, using and practicing reading skills, probably learning some new words here and there, and those skills will be ready and waiting if and when she decides to switch to something more substantive. It's good news that some of the romantic Beverly Cleary books are being reissued in paperback for middle-grade readers.

Good Books for Middle Readers
Series

THE BORROWERS
by Mary Norton
Harcourt, 1953; Harcourt paperback
■   The Lilliputian-like people who live under the grandfather clock earned their name from their habit of "borrowing" things from the big people who reside in the house, and putting them to their own uses. Tiny but very real characters. Sequels: *The Borrowers Afield*; *The Borrowers Afloat*; *The Borrowers Aloft*.

THE CHILDREN OF GREEN KNOWE
by Lucy M. Boston
illustrated by Peter Boston
Harcourt, 1959
■   Tolly visits Green Knowe, where his great-grandmother lives, and discovers the children who once lived there, too — in the seventeenth century! Exquisitely written. Others: *A Stranger at Green Knowe*; *The Treasure at Green Knowe*; *A River at Green Knowe*; *An Enemy at Green Knowe*.

ENCYCLOPEDIA BROWN, BOY DETECTIVE
by Donald J. Sobol
illustrated by Leonard Shortall
Nelson, 1963; Bantam paperback
■ Lightweight sleuthing is carried on by a ten-year-old detective. There are many, many sequels.

LITTLE HOUSE IN THE BIG WOODS
by Laura Ingalls Wilder
illustrated by Garth Williams
Harper, 1932; Harper paperback
■ With matchless prose and fascinating details, Mrs. Wilder tells of her girlhood days pioneering in America. Others: *Little House on the Prairie*; *On the Banks of Plum Creek*; *By the Shores of Silver Lake*; *Little Town on the Prairie*; *Farmer Boy*; *These Happy Golden Years*.

THE NARNIA CHRONICLES
by C. S. Lewis
Macmillan, 1950; Macmillan paperback
■ The first book in the series tells how four English children find that the back of a closet leads into a land where it is always winter, due to the spell of an evil White Witch. Series titles: *The Lion, the Witch, and the Wardrobe*; *Prince Caspian, The Return to Narnia*; *The Silver Chair*; *The Voyage of the Dawn Treader*; *The Magician's Nephew*; *The Last Battle*.

PRYDAIN CHRONICLES
by Lloyd Alexander
Holt, 1964; Dell paperback
■ In the imaginary land of Prydain, Taran, an assistant pigkeeper with dreams of glory, suddenly finds himself involved in battles on the side of the good Prince Gwydion to save his country from the forces of evil. An intriguing fantasy cycle, inspired by Welsh mythology. Series titles: *The Book of Three*; *The Black Cauldron*; *The Castle of Llyr*; *Taran Wanderer*. Also by Alexander: *Time Cat*; *The Marvelous Misadventures of Sebastian*.

Individual Titles

ABEL'S ISLAND
written and illustrated by William Steig
Farrar, 1976; Bantam paperback

■   Abel, a sheltered, well-to-do mouse, is swept from the side of his bride by a terrible storm and ends up Crusoe-like on a desert island, where he must use his wits to survive. A remarkable fantasy enhanced by Steig's line drawings and his eloquent literary style. Also: *Gorky Rises*; *Dominic*.

From *Abel's Island*.
Illustration by
William Steig.

ARE YOU THERE, GOD? IT'S ME, MARGARET
by Judy Blume
Bradbury, 1970; Dell paperback

■   The concerns of Margaret are what religion she should practice and whether or not she'll ever get her period. Set in middle-class suburbia, Blume's story is told with much humor. Also: *Blubber*; *Deenie*; *Iggie's House*; *It's Not the End of the World*; *Otherwise Known as Sheila the Great*; *Starring Sally J. Freedman as Herself*; *Then Again, Maybe I Won't*.

CALL IT COURAGE
by Armstrong Sperry
Macmillan, 1941; Macmillan paperback

■   Frightened by the sea ever since his mother drowned, Mafatu, a boy of the South Sea islands, finds the strength within himself to face his fear and conquer it.

BOOKS FOR MIDDLE GRADERS

THE CAT ATE MY GYMSUIT
by Paula Danziger
Delacorte, 1974; Dell paperback

■   An overweight thirteen-year-old girl feels unattractive and angry until
she meets a teacher who helps her sort things out. Told with much
humor and warmth. Also by Danziger: *Can You Sue Your Parents for
Malpractice?*; *There's a Bat in Bunk Five.*

DEAR MR. HENSHAW
by Beverly Cleary
Morrow, 1983

■   A touching account of a boy dealing with the divorce of his parents, a
new school, and his desire to express his feelings. Told in a series of letters and diary entries, this book is insightful as well as funny.

From
Dear Mr. Henshaw.
Illustration by
Paul O. Zelinsky.

DRAGONWINGS
by Lawrence Yep
Harper, 1975; Harper paperback

■   In the early part of this century, a Chinese boy moves to this country
to be with his father — and becomes involved in his father's great
dream of inventing a flying machine. For the mature reader. Also: *The
Mark Twain Murders*; *Sweetwater.*

FROM THE MIXED-UP FILES OF MRS. BASIL E. FRANKWEILER
by E. L. Konigsburg
Atheneum, 1967; Atheneum paperback

■ Two children run away to an unusual setting — New York City's Metropolitan Museum of Art. Also by Konigsburg: *Jennifer, Hecate, Macbeth, William McKinley and Me, Elizabeth; About the B'nai Bagels; Altogether, One at a Time; Father's Arcane Daughter; George.*

THE GREAT GILLY HOPKINS
by Katharine Paterson
Harper, 1978; Avon paperback

■ Gilly is an angry eleven-year-old foster child, striking out against the unfair shake she's gotten from life. But she meets her match in foster mother Maime Trotter and at last understands that she can love and be loved. Others by Paterson: *Bridge to Terabithia; The Master Puppeteer; Angels and Other Strangers; Of Nightingales That Weep; The Sign of the Chrysanthemum; Jacob Have I Loved.*

HARRIET THE SPY
by Louise Fitzhugh
Harper, 1964; Dell paperback

■ An eleven-year-old girl, whose parents just haven't the time to deal with her, creates a world for herself in a notebook of "spy" activities on her school friends and neighbors. Also by Fitzhugh: *The Long Street; Nobody's Family Is Going to Change.*

THE HOUSE WITH A CLOCK IN ITS WALLS
by John Bellairs
illustrated by Edward Gorey
Dial, 1973; Dell paperback

■ Orphaned Lewis goes to live with his Uncle Jonathan, who's a real wizard and lives in a huge old house with secret passageways and an eerie ticking within the walls. Lewis begins to dabble in magic himself to great effect. Fun and chills for buffs of the supernatural. Also by Bellairs: *The Figure in the Shadows; The Letter, the Witch, and the Ring; The Treasure of Alpheus Winterborn.*

BOOKS FOR MIDDLE GRADERS

THE HOUSE OF DIES DREAR
by Virginia Hamilton
illustrated by Eros Keith
Macmillan, 1968; Dell paperback

■ Ghosts from the days of the Underground Railroad seemingly come to life when a black family moves into the mysterious house once owned by Dies Drear. Another by Hamilton for this age group: *Zeely*; for a mature reader, *M. C. Higgins the Great*.

THE INDIAN IN THE CUPBOARD
by Lynne Reid Banks
illustrated by Brock Cole
Doubleday, 1980; Avon paperback

■ Omri, age 9 and the youngest of three brothers, finds that he can magically bring plastic "action figures" to life by placing them in an old cupboard. The thrill of it all is balanced by the realization of the huge responsibility of caring for a small, but nonetheless human, being.

From *Jacob Two-Two
Meets The Hooded Fang*.
Illustration by Fritz Wegner.

JACOB TWO-TWO MEETS THE HOODED FANG
by Mordecai Richler
Knopf, 1975; Bantam paperback

■ Jacob Two-Two (who has to say everything two times in his big family before anyone will pay any attention to him) accidentally insults a grownup and is sent to a vile children's prison for his crime in this whimsical, satirical fantasy.

THE MOFFATS
by Eleanor Estes
illustrated by Louis Slobodkin
Harcourt, 1941

■   Kids today still like the stories of the Moffat family, who don't have much money but have a lot of fun and enjoy each other. Others: *The Middle Moffat*; *Rufus M.* Also by Estes: *The Hundred Dresses*.

THE MIDNIGHT FOX
by Betsy Byars
illustrated by Ann Grifalconi
Viking, 1968; Avon paperback

■   A black fox is befriended and protected by a boy from the city who is summering in the country. Also by Byars: *The Pinballs*; *The Summer of the Swans*; *The TV Kid*; *The Night Swimmers*; *The Two-Thousand Pound Goldfish*; *The Cybil War*.

MRS. FRISBY AND THE RATS OF NIMH
by Robert C. O'Brien
illustrated by Zena Bernstein
Atheneum, 1971

■   In distress because of her sick child, Mrs. Frisby, a mouse, becomes involved with a group of rats who are on the verge of forming an advanced civilization thanks to their stint as lab rats, which endowed them with superintelligence.

From *Mrs. Frisby and the Rats of NIMH*. Illustration by Zena Bernstein.

NOTHING'S FAIR IN FIFTH GRADE
by Barthe DeClements
Viking, 1981; Scholastic paperback

■ In her fifth-grade year, Jenny finds difficulties which include dealing with multiplying and dividing fractions and with her conflicting feelings about a new girl in school who is terribly fat and gets caught stealing lunch money. DeClements really understands fifth-grade concerns.

From *The Phantom Tollbooth*.
Illustration by Jules Feiffer.

THE PHANTOM TOLLBOOTH
by Norton Juster
illustrated by Jules Feiffer
Random, 1961; Random paperback

■ For kids just discovering the joys of puns and double meanings, no book could be more perfect. Milo goes through a tollbooth, much as Alice went down the rabbit hole, and finds himself in strange lands with a logic all their own, populated by people such as the shortest tall man in the world and the tallest short man in the world, who are exactly the same size. Kids find this very, very funny.

BOOKS FOR MIDDLE GRADERS

TUCK EVERLASTING
by Natalie Babbitt
Farrar, 1975; Bantam paperback
■ After Winnie Foster meets the members of the Tuck family, who possess the secret of everlasting life, she has a big choice to make. Others by Babbitt: *The Search for Delicious*; *Knee-Knock Rise*; *Goody Hall*; *The Devil's Storybook*; *The Eyes of the Amaryllis*; *The Something*.

A WRINKLE IN TIME
by Madeline L'Engle
Farrar, 1962
■ Three children find a way to travel to another planet in a science fiction story that leaves kids pondering problems of our own world. For the excellent reader. Sequels: *A Wind in the Door*; *A Swiftly Tilting Planet*. Also: *A Ring of Endless Light*; *Meet the Austins*.

CONCLUSION

PICKING OUT GOOD BOOKS FOR KIDS is only the first step, of course. The next step is *sharing* those books with your children.

Remember, it's never too early to begin reading to your infant or too late to start reading aloud to your teenager. It is often helpful to pick a certain time of day — or night — that is designated as reading time, and to try to read regularly at this hour, no matter how many dishes are piled up in the kitchen sink or how many teeth have yet to be brushed. Some families like to read a bit before going off to school or work in the morning. I find this a hectic time in our house, so I prefer the traditional bedtime reading. What's important is that the time be considered a priority time.

I have many good memories of being read to as a child. I remember my mother and me laughing over *Winnie the Pooh* as Pooh and Piglet attempted to capture a Heffalump, and I remember crying with her one winter afternoon as *Little Women*'s Beth lay dying. I remember sitting spellbound at my desk after lunch in fifth grade as our teacher, Miss Smith, read to us each day from *A Tale of Two Cities*. My girlfriends and I all fell madly in love with Sydney Carton, and he became the noble standard by which we judged our fifth-grade boyfriends.

As I look back at the good books and the characters that have stayed with me through the years, I realize that I remember most of all the moments of laughter, the tears, the love — the emotions welling up from the stories and the intimate experience of sharing them with people I cared about. And it is this warm context for sharing stories, along with the stories themselves, that I hope to pass on as I read good books to my child.

Resources for Parents

Subject Guides

A TO ZOO: SUBJECT ACCESS TO CHILDREN'S PICTURE BOOKS
by Carolyn W. Lima
R. R. Bowker, 1982
- Any topic you can think of is listed in this guide. All entries are picture books, so they are suitable for young children, but neither annotations nor age ranges within the picture-book span are provided.

SUBJECT GUIDE TO CHILDREN'S BOOKS IN PRINT
R. R. Bowker, 1983
- A useful reference for finding currently in-print books by subject.

Books

BABIES NEED BOOKS
by Dorothy Butler
Atheneum, 1980
- Butler writes passionately and enchantingly about sharing books with young children, from birth until age 6. She includes many specific suggestions for books, with annotations.

THE BEST IN CHILDREN'S BOOKS: THE UNIVERSITY OF CHICAGO GUIDE TO CHILDREN'S LITERATURE
edited by Zena Sutherland
University of Chicago Press, 1980
- This is a collection of reviews from the *Bulletin of the Center for Children's Books.*

CHILDREN'S LITERATURE IN THE ELEMENTARY SCHOOL, THIRD EDITION
by Charlotte Huck and Doris Young Kuhn
Holt, 1979

■ Used as a text in college children's literature courses for teachers throughout the country, this big book backs up its plot summaries of good books with the latest pedagogical research. Amply illustrated.

CHOOSING BOOKS FOR CHILDREN: A COMMONSENSE GUIDE
by Betsy Hearne
Delacorte, 1981

■ Peppered with warm, personal anecdotes about children, books, and reading, Hearne's book is a joy to read and offers much practical advice.

ON LEARNING TO READ
by Bruno Bettelheim and Karen Zelan
Knopf, 1981

■ A condemnation of the reading practices used in our schools and recommendations on what we can do about it. Much food for thought for those concerned with children's reading.

A PARENT'S GUIDE TO CHILDREN'S READING: FIFTH EDITION
by Nancy Larrick
Bantam, 1982

■ A comprehensive guide on sharing literature with children, including annotated lists of books organized under useful headings, such as, "History — Fact and Fiction" and "Science and Nature."

RAISING READERS: A GUIDE TO SHARING LITERATURE WITH YOUNG CHILDREN
by Linda Leonard Lamme with Vivian Cox, Jane Matanzo, and Miken Olson
Walker, 1980

■ Many suggestions on how to share books with young kids and a long list of books to read, with annotations.

RESOURCES

THE READ-ALOUD HANDBOOK
by Jim Trelease
Penguin, 1979
- A bestseller, this guide to good books for reading aloud also gives a convincing argument for making reading aloud an established and enjoyable practice in the home.

THE USES OF ENCHANTMENT
by Bruno Bettelheim
Knopf, 1976
- Subtitled *The Meaning and Importance of Fairy Tales,* Bettelheim's book discusses the deep psychological significance of specific fairy tales and explains their importance to children's lives.

Magazines and Newsletters

THE CALENDAR
from The Children's Book Council, Inc.
67 Irving Place, New York, NY 10003
- The Book Council publishes *The Calendar* four times each year to provide information about current children's books.

THE HORN BOOK
Park Square Bldg.
31 St. James Avenue, Boston, MA 02116
- Published six times each year, *The Horn Book* is devoted to children's literature. It contains articles both of general interest and of scholarly interest in the field.

PARENTS' CHOICE
Parents' Choice Foundation
Box 185, Waban, MA 02168
- Contained here are reviews of books and, in addition, TV shows, movies, tapes, records, toys, and games for kids.

Pamphlets

CHILDREN'S BOOKS
Office of Children's Services
New York Public Library
8 East 40th Street, New York, NY 10016

■ This pamphlet offers an annotated list of the one hundred books published each year that are considered the best by a committee of experienced librarians. For a copy, send $1.50 to the address above. Make checks payable to Office of Branch Libraries.

CHILDREN'S CHOICES
International Reading Association
P.O. Box 8139, Newark, DE 19711

■ Each year, under the auspices of the International Reading Association and the Children's Book Council, teams of children — five teams of approximately two thousand children per team — read new children's books that are published and vote on their favorites. It's a great list to have if you're looking for material to motivate your reader. Single copies are available free from the address above. Send a self-addressed stamped envelope with enough postage for two ounces, first class.

INDEX TO TITLES

INDEX